Developing Creativity

90 Minute Guides

Michelle N. Halsey

Silver City Publications & Training, L.L.C.
P.O. Box 1914
Nampa, ID 83653
https://www.silvercitypublications.com/shop/

ISBN-10: 1-64004-016-1
ISBN-13: 978-1-64004-016-8

Contents

Chapter 1 – Getting Started

Creativity and innovation will improve your chances of success in business and in life. Fortunately, there are steps that can be taken to inspire you and develop your creative mindset. By changing the way that you think and overcoming your fear of risk, you will improve you creativity and change your life. Implementing the guidelines in this module is the first step to forever changing your creative process.

Research has consistently demonstrated that when clear goals are associated with learning, it occurs more easily and rapidly. With that in mind, let's review our goals for today.

At the end of this tutorial, participants should be able to:

- Define creativity

- Act with confidence

- Engage in curiosity

- Stop acting out of fear

- Learn from introspection

- Take risks

Chapter 2 – What is Creativity?

There are different types of creativity, which makes it difficult to define. People often limit their definitions of creativity to art, but this is too limiting. Creativity comes in the form of original thought, divergent thinking, problem solving, inspiration, and imagination. In order to improve creativity, it is essential that you understand the definition of creative thinking and what steps you can take to improve your own thought process.

Divergent Thinking

Divergent thinking moves away from the traditional, convergent thinking, which is linear and analytical. It is looking for the right answer. Divergent thinking, on the other hand, is nonlinear and spontaneous. Rather than finding a single correct answer, the divergent thinker discovers multiple options for addressing problems. Brainstorming, predicting, and imagination activities are all examples of divergent thinking. It is possible to increase divergent thinking by implementing open-ended questions when addressing problems rather than closed questions. We will discuss open-ended questions in a later module. Moving toward divergent thinking may not be comfortable for analytical thinkers, but practice will soon help creativity develop.

Problem Solving

It is possible to improve the problem solving process by implementing creativity. This requires looking at each problem as a unique situation rather than applying the same principles to every similar problem.

Steps to Creative Problem Solving:

- View the problem in different ways.

- Do not make assumptions that all similar projects or problems are the same.

- Be open to different problem solving options.

- Look at the big picture when addressing problems.

- Keep looking even when the solution is not easily found.

Problem Solving Activity

In the space, apply the creative problem solving skills to something that you need to address in your work or personal life.

Imagination and Inspiration

Inspiration and imagination are essential for creativity. Webster defines imagination as the ability to "recombine the materials furnished by experience or memory, for the accomplishment of an elevated purpose; the power of conceiving and expressing the ideal." In the modern world, it is easy to ignore the development of the imagination, but this is done to your detriment. Exercising the imagination is necessary to improve creativity.

Ways to Improve Imagination:

- Read stories.

- Expose yourself to new experiences and influences.

- Get enough rest.

- Daydream and meditate.

Inspiration is what prompts creativity. Inspiration provides the motivation that helps people believe that they can or should do something creative; or inspiration can be an idea that comes suddenly. Inspiration is different for different people. There are ways to improve inspiration, which we will address in a later module.

Something Out of Nothing

Many people have pointed out that it is not physically possible to create something out of nothing. The idea of creating something out of nothing is creating something new or original. True creativity does more than take from the creativity of others, which is why we value originality. Although, it is possible to find creative ways to improve on what already exists. There is no single method or setting to create something new. From art to science to the office, you can create something in any area as long as you have the imagination and inspiration to develop new ideas.

Case Study

Steve was a logical person who prided himself on his problem solving skills. He focused on the convergent thinking and had tried and true methods he used in specific situations. A new project manager challenged the department to apply creative problem solving. Steve was unimpressed with the ideas, he was certain that his ways were best. The next month, his colleagues surprised him. Several of them came up with new ideas that he never considered. Steve decided to apply his imagination and look at problems in a different light. Over the course of the next few weeks, he was able to increase his productivity by discovering new ways of viewing problems.

Chapter 3 – Getting Inspired

Motivation and inspiration go hand in hand. When you are inspired, you increase your level of creativity. You should not simply wait for inspiration to find you. You need to get in touch with what you are passionate about and what inspires you. By finding ways to increase your inspiration, you will increase your creativity and help find the motivation that you need.

Introspection

Introspection is the process of self-examination, which helps people understand what inspires them. Introspective individuals are in tune with their feelings, thoughts, and what motivates their behavior. The art of introspection requires people to take the time to question what they want and how they feel, which is easy to overlook in today's fast paced society. Activities such as journaling and meditation will help facilitate the process of introspection. Once people become aware of their thoughts and feelings, they will be in a better position to increase their creativity and achieve their goals.

Introspection Activity

Take a few minutes to answer the following questions.

- Describe how you feel about your life.

- What do you want to achieve?

- What do you think about your life?

- Are there any thoughts or feelings you are ignoring?

Read More

Reading stimulates thinking and is an important tool to improve creativity. When choosing reading material, be sure to include fictional works because they engage the imagination. Look for stories that you find inspirational, and carve out the time to read them. Begin your reading regime by setting realistic goals. If goals are not realistic, you will not read more. You do not need to carve out hours of reading time. Simply set aside 15 minutes a day to read and find your inspiration.

Removing the Mental Block

Everyone faces mental blocks from time to time. These blocks will prevent focusing, finding answers to problems, discovering inspiration, and achieving goals. Overcoming mental blocks is difficult but it can be done. If you find yourself blocked, stop and refocus by doing something distracting. Consider the following techniques to refocus and overcome the mental blocks:

- A change of scenery (someplace relaxing or inspirational)

- Meditate

- Read

- Busy work

- Exercise

Mental Blocks

In the space, make a list of activities that you have found to help you overcome mental blocks in the past as well as activities you will try in the future.

Art Inspires Art

Art is inspirational, and throwing yourself into art will inspire your own creativity. Simply exposing yourself to random art is not enough to inspire you. You must find the art that speaks to you. Whether you choose photography, sculpture, painting, dance, theater, music, or computer graphics, there is something to inspire everyone. The art that inspires you does not need to be directly connected to what you do; it simply needs to be inspiring. Once you find the art forms that inspire you, immerse yourself in them. Listen to an inspirational song on the way to work or flip through pictures during lunch breaks.

Taking the time to immerse yourself in art will help you find the inspiration that you need to think creatively.

Case Study

Alice had difficulty finding inspiration for her new project. She tried to think creatively, but she was constantly distracted. A friend suggested that Alice go to the park and try to find some introspection. At first, Alice found the task awkward, but after a few minutes, she realized that she was not happy about the job and secretly did not want to do it. Additionally, she realized that she had not reached many of her goals in life and viewed herself as a failure. Once Alice realized all of the negativity that she brought to the project, she was able to address her own thoughts and feelings and refocus on the task at hand. She was able to present the best project she had ever done.

Chapter 4 – Beating Procrastination

Whether we are inspired or not, we will always have to fight procrastination. There are always distractions and excuses to prevent us from reaching our goals and keep us in the running behind schedule. Fortunately, there are steps that everyone can take to limit distractions and improve both the creative process and productivity.

Get Rid of Clutter

It may seem innocuous, but clutter has very real and damaging effects. It will increase stress and create distractions that damage your creative process while encouraging procrastination. Simply getting rid of unnecessary clutter is enough to prevent procrastination in many instances. Create a clutter free environment by removing all nonessential items from the workspace. This includes trash, old papers, and gadgets. You should feel free, however, to keep inspirational items such as art to encourage you in your own creative process.

Steps to being Clutter Free:

- Remove unnecessary items.

- Clean up the area at the end of each workday.

- Keep everything organized and put things back where they go.

- Do not allow other people to clutter up your office.

- Have space chosen for items before you bring them into your work area.

Self-Imposed Limitations

Procrastination is often caused by limitations that we place on ourselves, the hidden belief that we are not capable of reaching our goals. The best way to break through these limitations is a change of mindset, look at the situation honestly, and create the situations that force you to act. For example, making public announcements or placing short deadlines will provide enough stress to increase adrenaline and create focus. It is important not to go overboard when creating stressful situations. While short deadlines will increase adrenaline, impossible deadlines will only create a cycle of failure, which leads to further procrastination.

Self-Imposed Limitations Activity

Make a list of projects that you have been procrastinating on completing.

- _____

- _____

- _____

- _____

Make a short but achievable deadline for each one.

_____

_____

_____

_____

Build on Small Successes

When attempting to decrease procrastination and motivate yourself to move forward, it is essential that you focus on success. The best way to accomplish this is by setting small goals that you know you can achieve such as reading for 10 or 15 minutes a day or walking for a short time before work. If you begin with activities that you know you can achieve, you will create an environment of success. Encouraged by your own achievements, you will be able to slowly build on your success until you reach your long-term goals. When you believe that it is possible to complete a task, you will be less likely to procrastinate on your work.

Small Successes Exercises

Write a list of goals that you can easily achieve:

- _____

- _____

- _____

- _____

- _____

- _____

- _____

- _____

Don't Start at the Beginning

When you are thinking creatively, it is not necessary to complete tasks in a linear manner. Sometimes the beginning of a project is the most difficult. Rather than getting stuck at the beginning, move on to a portion of the project that you can complete and go back to the beginning later. For example, many writers choose to leave the introductions to their stories at the very end and tie all of the events together. It does not matter where you begin in the project as long as you are able to connect all of the portions of the project together.

Case Study

Jennifer had goals and ideas, but she found herself constantly procrastinating. She would become momentarily distracted only to find herself looking at the clock to see 20 minutes had passed since she looked away from the task at hand. After talking to her mentor, she decided to remove the clutter from her workspace. She took organized her office so that everything had a place. She removed some of the toys and gadgets that she found distracting. She did keep a motivational poster, but everything else in the office was work related. The first week was difficult, but Jennifer was able to see progress after a while. Soon, she was spurred on by her own success.

Chapter 5 — Improving Your Creative Mindset

Developing a creative mindset takes time and work. Developing creativity requires flexibility and the ability to move away from rigid thought patterns than blind us from taking advantage of new ways to improve creativity. Changing the way that you view the world may not be comfortable at first, but it is worth the reward.

Open Mind

Creativity requires keeping an open mind when faced with ideas that you do not agree with. Many people assume they are open-minded but have strong, negative emotional responses when they are faced with views that do not line up with theirs. Keeping an open mind demands understanding your own belief system, this is easier to do when you have introspection. Having an open mind does not mean that you have to change your own beliefs; you simply have to try to listen to other points of view without automatically shutting people out. It is possible that you will find common ground with people who disagree with you and be able to learn from opposing points of view. After all, you do not know everything.

Do Not Judge

Part of keeping an open mind requires refraining from making judgments. The speed with which information travels in the digital age seems to encourage people to pass emotional judgments before they have all of the facts. It is easy to see people as two-dimensional tropes or stereotypes based on a single opinion. Rather than making snap decisions about people and viewing the world as black and white, take the time to appreciate different points of view and ideas. Just because someone believes something that you do not, does not make that person evil or the enemy. Do not make the mistake of allowing personal bias to keep you from learning something new or developing relationships that will empower your creativity.

Positive Mindset

Remaining positive is essential to the creative mindset and in everything we do. It is easy to focus on the negative aspects of life because we are hardwired to remember negative information, but this will only lead to depression and self-fulfilling prophecies of failure. There are ways to improve positivity and change your mindset so that you can become more successful in whatever you do.

- **Count your blessings:** Focus on the things that you have to be thankful for in your life. You may want to keep a daily list of good things to pull your attention away from the negative.

- **Use positive affirmations:** This may seem strange at first, but positive affirmations will help you truly believe that the best is possible.

- **Confront negative thoughts:** When facing difficult times, place the events in perspective. It is easy to overreact. Facing the situation directly and honestly will prevent an unhealthy focus on the negative.

Affirmations

Write down a few affirmations that you can use to create a positive mindset.

Ask Why?

As we have already noted, rushing to snap decisions and judgments will actually hinder creative thought. Rather than accepting everything at face value, it is better to question. Questioning will increase creativity. It is important to question everything and get as many answers as possible. Find different opinions from different people, and explore the answers that they provide. Taking the time to find the answers will prevent any unnecessary confusion and allow you to see things from a different perspective, which will increase your creativity.

Case Study

Marjorie was extremely opinionated. She knew what she believed and she had no problem letting people know when they were wrong, at least in her opinion. Her boss told her that she might learn more if she were open minded and less judgmental, but Marjorie already considered him to be an overly emotional fool who was not always rational. She ignored his advice, and continued to alienate the people around her. Many employees fled her department. Soon, she was only working with people who viewed the world exactly as she did. Her department eventually lagged behind the others, and her boss told her that they lacked creativity.

The ability to think creatively and change your mindset requires you to make discoveries and associations. It is necessary to question, be self-aware, and develop confidence in order to increase your creative thought. Following the instructions in this module will help you improve your creativity and reach your full potential.

Make Associations

People naturally make associations. In creative thinking, it is useful to make unusual associations such as tasks, ideas, and items that seem to be unrelated. One method for accomplishing this is trying to create forced associations. This is a useful brainstorming tool where lists of unrelated concepts are created. The individuals or groups then make connections between two or more unrelated ideas at a time. The exercise is difficult at first, but creating unusual associations will begin to build creativity with time and practice.

Keep a Journal

Keeping a journal allows you to develop creativity and track your progress. People who fail in journaling often make the process too complicated. Keeping a journal should be a simple and personal process. There are different ways to keep journals, and you need to choose the one that fits your needs. You may choose from the traditional methods, keeping one on the computer, and there are even apps for journaling. Once you choose the method of journaling that is best for you, follow these simple directions.

Keeping a Journal:

- **Choose the right time**: Pick the time of day when you will have the time and motivation to journal.

- **Choose the spot**: Find the place where you will feel comfortable and inspired.

- **Be comfortable**: Do not place too much stress on yourself. A journal does not have to be perfectly written and should address the topics that you find relevant.

Journal

Answer the following questions to help begin the journaling process.

- Which method of journaling would you prefer?

- Where is a good place to journal?

- What time of day is best for you to make journal entries?

Question Assumptions

We all make assumptions, which are concepts that we believe without proof. They are based on personal experience to help us understand the world around us. Unfortunately, accepting assumptions without question will cause problems in the way that we view the world and other people, which decrease creativity. It is essential to question assumptions when they are encountered. Simply ask the following questions:

- What is the assumption?

- What if it not true?

- How does this assumption affect my decision-making?

Once you understand how an assumption affects your decision making skills, consider other points of view, and look for evidence that you may have overlooked when creating your assumption.

Assumptions

Think of one assumption you have and ask yourself the following questions:

What is the assumption?

_____

_____

What if it is not true?

_____

_____

How does this assumption affect my decision-making?

_____

_____

Creative Confidence

Confidence is the key to success in any activity. If you believe that you can do something, you are more likely to complete it well, and creative tasks are no exception. Unfortunately, it is easy to lose confidence in creative ability because of self-comparison. When it comes to building your creative confidence, it is important that you are guided by your inspiration.

Steps to Building Creative Confidence:

- Focus on your achievements.

- Play to your strengths.

- Stay positive.

- Create what speaks to you.

Being confident will help you realize that you can do whatever you set your mind to do.

Case Study

Ginny had tried journaling before, but she always gave up after a few weeks. She found the process time consuming and intimidating. She spent so much time self-editing that she did not find the activity helpful. Ginny began a new program at work that encouraged regular journaling. She decided to give it one last try and downloaded an app to help her. She also gave up trying to be insightful and simply recorded her thoughts and feelings. After all, she wasn't writing it to be published or read by strangers. After a few weeks, she realized that journaling had become second nature to her.

Additionally, Ginny discovered that it became easier for her to recall her thoughts and feelings. Her new self-awareness helped her change her mindset and improver her creativity. After six months, the company was using some of her creative ideas, and revenue was up by 15%.

Chapter 6 – Curiosity

Curiosity is a trait that people typically associate with children. Curiosity, however, is a trait that we should all cultivate. A lack of curiosity is associated with depression. People who engage and cultivate curiosity are happier and more creative than those who do not. By taking the steps to improve curiosity, you will also improve your own creative process.

Spark Your Curiosity

The human brain responds to rewards. We are not likely to repeat behavior if we do not see the benefit, which is why rewarding curiosity is necessary to spark it. Look for intrinsic and extrinsic motivations that will help you on the road to pique your curiosity. The reward of satisfying curiosity is an example of intrinsic motivation. Extrinsic motivation is an external reward. Gamification, which borrows from gaming theory, is a useful tool to reward your curiosity.

- **Choose tasks related to curiosity:** Make a list.

- **Assign points**: Assign a number of points to each task. Tasks that are more difficult should be given more points.

- **Assign rewards:** Better rewards have higher points attached to them. For example, a visit to a coffee shop could be 20 points, while buying an app could be 50 points. The rewards will depend on what motivates you.

- **Keep score:** Find a way to keep track of your points that works for you. You could use anything from spreadsheets to phone apps.

Game

Create a list of tasks to encourage creativity and assign points to them.

Task	Points

Curiosity is the Engine of Creativity

Curiosity is what motivates learning and creativity. We become curious when we desire to fill the knowledge gap and increase our understanding. Satisfying curiosity and improving a creative mindset requires mental and creative stimulation.

- Begin by asking questions regularly. Enjoy the questioning process, and do not rush to a conclusion.

- Learn something new every day, and use this information to pique curiosity.

- Communicate with people about topics that interest you so that you can both learn new information and teach.

Engage

It is easy to believe the stereotype that creative people are always solitary. In reality, however, human interaction is important in encouraging curiosity and increasing creativity. We need people for our physical and mental well-being. Rather than being locked away in creative pursuits, take the time to engage with others. Talk to people, share your expertise, and join different groups to build relationships.

How to Engage:

- Ask questions.

- Get to know people; do not push relationships.

- Keep old friends as you make new ones.

- Connect over shared passions and ideas.

Ask Open-Ended Questions

As we have already stated open-ended questions are useful for increasing creativity. Unlike closed questions, which have specific correct answers, open-ended questions are broad need to be explored. These questions should be familiar from essay questions in high school.

Open-ended question example:

"What are the different ways of looking at the situation?"

Open-ended questions develop curiosity because they allow you to explore the topic instead of rushing straight to find the answer.

Case Study

Heath always tried to reach conclusions as quickly as possible. He liked concrete knowledge rather than abstract thought. When working on his most recent project, he became frustrated because he could not find the answer to his questions. He began to resent the project and the topic in general. A friend suggested that increasing his curiosity in the subject and working with others might help him find the answers he needed. Heath chose to develop a support team, but he was skeptical. The team shared their ideas and explored questions. The group had difficulty melding at first, but they soon learned to appreciate each other. Heath was surprised at how much he did not know and found himself interested in discovering more. The project ended better than he expected it to be.

Chapter 7 – Take Risks

There is no certain success when it comes to creativity. Every creative endeavor requires taking a risk. Developing creativity demands that you face your fears and act with confidence. Learning to accept yourself and ignore harmful criticism will give you the strength and confidence that you need to take the risks that creativity demands.

Be Confident

Being confident is a delicate balance that many people have difficulty keeping. On the one hand, overconfidence can lead to arrogance that causes individuals to view themselves as better or more important than other people. On the other hand, a lack of confidence causes self-doubt that will hinder creativity. Confidence is a natural state when you believe in yourself.

Steps to Creating Confidence:

- **Trust yourself**: Believe that you will be able to learn, grow, and accomplish your goals.

- **Leave your comfort zone**: Taking risks and trying new things will show you that you are capable of more than you realize.

- **Accept praise**: Be comfortable with well-deserved praise, but do not demand it. Refusing praise is not the same thing as humility.

Scared to Fail?

Fear of failure is more damaging than failure itself. Living in fear keeps our lives in holding patterns and we never grow. There is no reason to be afraid of failure because it is inevitable. If, however, we are able to view failure as a learning opportunity, then we can become comfortable with the idea and learn to take risks. When we are willing to take risks without fear, we open ourselves to opportunities that we would have overlooked, and we come closer to achieving our dreams.

Steps to Overcome Fear:

- Embrace mistakes

- Do not over think your plans

- Say yes to opportunities that you truly want

- Accept advice and help

Fake It Till You Make It

The old saying fake it till you make it is actually sound advice. From a psychological point of view, acting with the self-confidence that you want will actually help increase your confidence. If you believe that you can do something, you create a self-fulfilling prophecy. The greater your belief, the more likely you are to succeed.

Steps:

- Dress the part that you want to play.

- Relax and smile.

- Be aware of your body and posture.

- Use the appropriate vocabulary.

Opportunities

Make a list of things you would do or opportunities you would take without a fear of failure.

- _____

- _____

- _____

- _____

- _____

Afraid to Be Judged

Fear of failure often coincides with fear of judgment. This is nothing to fear because it is inevitable. People are judgmental, and you will face unfair criticism. You cannot allow this to control you. If you do, the fear will block your creativity. Learning to ignore naysayers and accept yourself will give you the strength to accept risks.

- **Assess how judgmental you are**: Not judging others will help you find perspective when you are judged.

- **Look at yourself honestly**: If you are honest with yourself, you will be able to discern constructive criticism from judgment.

- **Value yourself**: Your self-worth does not come from other people.

Overcoming the fear of judgment may require changing your mindset, but it is worth the effort.

Judgment

Make a list of things you would do or opportunities you would take without a fear of judgment.

- _____

- _____

- _____

- _____

- _____

- _____

- _____

Case Study

Theresa was an accomplished dancer, but she never performed for people. She made a mistake at a recital once and never forgot the humiliation. Afraid of making a mistake again, she chose to only dance in private, which meant that she could never have a career in her passion. She continued to practice when she wasn't working in an office. One day, a coworker suggested that she perform in a televised talent show. Part of Theresa wanted to do it, but the other part of her did not want to take the risk.

As she honestly assessed her past failure, however, she realized that she overreacted. She paid too much attention to people who made fun of her and never learned from the fall. She decided to take a chance and perform again. Theresa chose to perform for herself and not take her sense of worth from a group of strangers.

Chapter 8 – Think Like a Child

Children are naturally creative. Unfortunately, we lose some of this creativity as we grow up. We lose our curiosity and forget to daydream and play. When we forget to have fun, we forget to be creative. By remembering how to think like a child, we activate our creativity. While it may seem counterintuitive, thinking like a child will make living as an adult easier and more enjoyable.

Daydream

Everyone daydreams; it is natural. As children, many of us are taught that daydreaming is a waste time that distracts us from important activities. Daydreaming, however, is actually a useful tool that the mind needs. Biologically, the act of daydreaming is similar to dreaming or meditating. It shifts the parts of the brain being used, and aids both in relaxation and alleviating monotony. Occasionally allowing the mind to wander can actually increase productivity as people clear their minds and refocus. Additionally, daydreams connect us with our goals and desires. They inspire us to act on our dreams because we have already pictured them as reality.

While daydreaming is useful, it is important not to go overboard. Allow yourself small chunks of time (15 minute maximum) to daydream. The point is to allow yourself a break so that you activate creativity and return to work with a better focus.

Be Curious

We have already spent an entire module addressing the importance of curiosity. It will be easier for us to reignite our curiosity when we remember the time in our lives when we are the most curious, childhood. The world is a marvelous place for children who regularly ask why or how. Familiar questions include "Why is the sky blue?" and "How does it work?" A certain joy comes from asking questions and pursuing their answers. Children are not afraid to ask questions because they believe that they can find the answers. Adults often discourage this type of questioning, but discouragement only hinders creativity.

Activate your curiosity by considering what interests you and why some things work while others do not. Ask questions like a child would, and you will find your curiosity increasing.

Curiosity

Write a list of questions that are relevant to you, and ask them the way that you would have as a child.

- _____
- _____
- _____
- _____
- _____

Play Games

We all need to take more time to play, and games are the perfect way to connect with our inner child. People enjoy games, which is why the number of games available for smartphones keeps increasing. Games are useful motivators that keep our minds sharp and improve our creativity. Making games a part of our daily routine will inspire and motivate us to reach our goals. We have already discussed using gamification to motivate work, but this should not be the only game that you play. It is important to participate in a variety of games to stimulate different thought processes.

For example, chess teaches logic and strategy, video games are tied to increased creativity, and puzzle games are known to improve mental function. Try different games until you find the ones that appeal to you. If you do not enjoy a game, you are not likely to play it.

Experiment

Children are fascinated when they encounter something new. As adults, however, our fascination is more likely to be hesitation. Adults develop routines and safe zones. Part of taking risks and living creatively, however, requires us to experiment and try new things. Trying something new prevents boredom and forces us to grow and expand our horizons. Rather than getting stuck in a safe, controlled environment, learn to say yes to new experiences. This is not an excuse to be reckless and make bad decisions; it is simply a reminder that there is always more to experience in life.

Experiment with new food, go to places you don't normally frequent, take classes, and meet new people. You will not enjoy everything you try, but you will never be bored, and you may discover new inspiration to spark your creativity.

Case Study

Darla was a bookkeeper who never varied from her routine. She kept the same schedule, drove the same routes, ate the same food, and talked to the same people every day. As boring as her life was, Darla was uncomfortable with the idea of change. For her New Year's resolution, she decided to try something new and indulge her creative side. She took dance lessons, which she always too afraid to try. After a few weeks, she discovered that she enjoyed dancing, and she was better at it than she thought she would be. Additionally, she met new people in the group, and they would go out after their lesson. One of her new friends owned an art gallery and was a looking for a bookkeeper. Darla believed that she was ready for another change.

Chapter 9 – Environmental Factors

The environment you work in affects your creativity. Fortunately, there are steps you can take to control of your environment and develop creativity. Make your work area inspiring, go to locations that increase creativity and take care of yourself to increase your creative mindset. Following the information outlined in this module will help improve your creativity.

Work Area

Your work area should be a reflection of you. You may not have complete control of the décor at work, but there are steps that you can take to help make the area more inspiring. Recall places that you find inspiring, and add small touches to recreate that inspiration. Fill the workspace with items that inspire you such as pictures or books. This could include pictures of your family or places that you stir emotion in you. Just make sure that you do not use the need for inspiration as an excuse to bring unneeded clutter into your environment. The workspace should be clean and organized in order for you to be the most productive. Inspiring work areas are different for different people. Some people prefer whimsy and other clean lines. Simply choose what inspires you.

Additional Environments

Your workspace is not the only space that can increase your creativity. You should consider adding additional environments to help inspire your creativity. These locations have atmosphere that you find inspiring. These places could be coffee shops, parks, museums, etc. If you do not have any additional environments, consider visiting different places in the city so that you can find some. Different environments will inspire different emotions. Having additional environments allows you to fine tune the inspiration that you receive. Once you identify these environments, you know where you can go to soak up some inspiration.

Additional Environments

Make a list of places that you find inspiring. Explain which emotion these places inspire in you.

Get Enough Sleep

Getting enough sleep is common sense, but you may not know that sleep is an important component in the creative process. This is because dreaming is very important to the creative process, and you have to reach REM sleep to dream. Additionally, scientists have discovered that people are 33% more likely to connect ideas to each other after sleeping. Unfortunately, many of us, particularly in the United States do not get enough sleep. So, improve your creativity by adapting healthy sleep habits.

Sleep Habits:

- Stick to a schedule.

- Create a routine before bed to mentally prepare.

- Avoid alcohol, nicotine, and caffeine.

- Sleep in a dark and comfortable environment.

- Avoid computer, phone, and television screen because they can alter circadian rhythm.

Sleep Activity

Draft a bedtime ritual to help you mentally prepare for sleep.

Variables

When examining your environmental factors, remember there are many different variables to consider. A simple change of smell or color can flood a person with memories or create strong emotional responses. Whether you are changing your home environment or are assessing additional environments, you need to pay attention to these variables and understand exactly how they will affect your creative process.

Variables:

- Light

- Color

- Smell

- Sound

- Music

- Proximity to people

Experimenting with different variables will help you determine how to create the best environment to aid your creativity. The important thing to remember is that you feel safe and comfortable.

Case Study

Brian is known as a creative problem solver, but he has not been able to focus well lately. He is tired and distracted. He keeps hitting a wall trying to choose the direction in which to take the company. Brian is frustrated and tired. He stays up for days trying to make a decision before he calls his mentor who tells him to sleep on the decision. Brian thinks that the idea was too simplistic, but he is exhausted. He goes to bed early that night and sleeps. When he wakes up, the answer seems to suddenly appear. All of the connections make sense, and he is finally able to make his decision.

Chapter 10 – Individual Brainstorming

Most of us are familiar with brainstorming. Students practice it in school, and it is a popular technique in business environments. Brainstorming is used in lateral or divergent thinking and helps boost creative thinking. Individual brainstorming can be effective in your personal or business life. Following the tips in this module will help improve brainstorming and divergent thinking to increase creativity.

Generate A Lot of Ideas

Brainstorming does not require self-editing. The point is to generate as many ideas as possible. When you place the focus on the number of ideas rather than whether they are good or not, your mind will make connections that it normally would not when you do not place restrictions on it. You should write down every idea that comes to you. Before you brainstorm, choose a quiet place, and limit distractions. Focus on the problem that you need to address and begin writing. This technique may be familiar from free writing exercises in writing classes, where you write as many ideas as possible without changing anything that you write.

Brainstorm

Think of something that you need to address and brainstorm ideas using free writing.

Mind Mapping

Mind mapping can be done after ideas have been generated. Also known as concept mapping and spider mapping, the technique is use to organize information and ideas in the way that they relate to each other. You may write your own map or use software to help you map your ideas.

Begin by identifying the main ideas or concepts and arrange them. Next, connect the other ideas to the main concepts that they relate to using lines and linking words or descriptions. The map will continue to grow and does not have to end. It is possible that you with think of new ideas as you create the map. Feel free to include them.

Visualization

Visualization is a useful technique in different areas of life. In brainstorming sessions, visualization requires envisioning ideas that are brainstormed. You must visualize the different solutions to determine which ones will work best.

Visualization Steps:

- **Choose an idea or solution**: Visualization needs to be specific.

- **Relax**: Find a time and place to relax and focus on visualization techniques.

- **Visualize:** Picture the future in detail, and visualize it happening in the present down to the last detail.

After visualizing an idea, you should have a better idea about their effectiveness and suitability. You will be able to cross some ideas off your list after you visualize them.

Organize and Bring Ideas Together

The final step in the brainstorming process is to organize your ideas and bring them together. It is usually best to step away from the brainstorming before organizing your ideas. Take the ideas from the concept map that survived the visualization process and consider the best way to organize them. Consider how they are connected and if any of them can be combined into new ideas. Then, create a list of ideas to help guide you in the future. It is important that you do not limit yourself to these ideas; you should add to them regularly.

Case Study

Wendell hated brainstorming. The process made him nervous, and he never developed many ideas. In fact, most of the ideas he did come up with were repeats of earlier ideas. He did not understand why other people swore by the technique. Wendell met with his mentor who taught him the art of free writing. It took practice, but he was able to stop self-editing. He began listing ideas that he never would have considered before. He began to develop truly unique ideas in his brainstorming sessions. Soon, he was on a regular basis.

Additional Titles

The 90 Minute Guide series of books covers a variety of general business skills and are intended to be completed in 90 minutes or less. It is an effective way for building your skill set and can be used to acquire professional development units needed by project managers and other industries to maintain their certification. For the availability of titles please see

https://www.silvercitypublications.com/shop/.

No. 1 - Appreciative Inquiry

No. 2 - Assertiveness and Self Control

No. 3 - Attention Management

No. 4 - Body Language Basics

No. 5 - Business Acumen

No. 6 - Business and Etiquette

No. 7 - Change Management

No. 8 - Coaching and Mentoring

No. 9 - Communications Strategies

No. 10 - Conflict Resolution

No. 11 - Creative Problem Solving

No. 12 - Delivering Constructive Criticism

No. 13 - Developing Creativity

No. 14 - Developing Emotional Intelligence

No. 15 - Developing Interpersonal Skills

No. 16 - Developing Social Intelligence

No. 17 - Employee Motivation

No. 18 - Facilitation Skills

No. 19 - Goal Setting and Getting Things Done

No. 20 - Knowledge Management Fundamentals

No. 21 - Leadership and Influence

No. 22 - Lean Process and Six Sigma Basics

No. 23 - Managing Anger

No. 24 - Meeting Management

No. 25 - Negotiation Skills

No. 26 - Networking Inside a Company

No. 27 - Networking Outside a Company

No. 28 - Office Politics for Managers

No. 29 - Organizational Skills

No. 30 - Performance Management

No. 31 - Presentation Skills

No. 32 - Public Speaking

No. 33 - Servant Leadership

www.ingramcontent.com/pod-product-compliance
Lightning Source LLC
Chambersburg PA
CBHW060042040426

42331CB00032B/2181